101

THINGS

YOU

NEED TO

KNOW

Scholastic Inc.
New York Toronto London Auckland Sydney
Mexico City New Delhi Hong Kong Buenos Aires

P9-DYZ-202

Designed by Julie Mullarkey-Gnoy
Illustrated by Larry Ross
ISBN 0-439-56983-4

12 11 10 9 8 7 6 5 4 3 2 1   3 4 5 6 7 8/0

Printed in the U.S.A.
First printing, September 2003

What's the difference between heat and temperature?
How do you figure out the circumference of a circle?
Who made the first national flag? Where do you place the
colon in a business letter? Why do earthquakes happen?

Dive right in to *101 Things You Need to Know,* a quick
and easy-to-explore reference that is fact-filled plus
fun-filled . . . from Fact 1 to 101!

FACT 1

Betsy Ross could make a five-pointed star with one scissor cut! Impressed by her talent with scissors and cloth, George Washington asked her to make the first American flag.

On June 14, 1777, the Continental Congress adopted the national flag. It had thirteen stripes of alternating red and white. The thirteen stars were designed in a circle to represent equality among the thirteen colonies.

FACT 2

Meet the Nyms . . . Synonym, Antonym, and Homonym!

"Nym" is the Greek word for "name." Synonyms are words that mean exactly the same thing. Antonyms are words that mean exactly the opposite. Homonyms are words that sound the same but mean different things.

SYNONYMS	ANTONYMS	HOMONYMS
able/capable	sweet/bitter	ad/add
danger/hazard	buy/sell	beet/beat
help/aid	east/west	capital/capitol
method/way	fact/fiction	be/bee
start/begin	laugh/cry	groan/grown

The Five Longest Rivers in the World Are:

RIVER	CONTINENT	APPROX. LENGTH
1. **Nile**	Africa	4,160 miles
2. **Amazon**	South America	4,000 miles
3. **Yangtze** (Chang Jiang)	Asia	3,964 miles
4. **Mississippi-Missouri**	North America	3,808 miles
5. **Huang He** (or Yellow)	Asia	3,400 miles

Rivers are long bodies of water that flow over land. The source of the river is where most of its water comes from. The mouth of the river is where it empties into another large body of water.

FACT
4

Eggs-traordinary! The world's largest flightless bird is the ostrich. An ostrich's egg is equal in volume to 2 dozen chicken eggs!

OTHER BIRD FACT WORLD RECORDS

Fastest Flyer: peregrine falcon

Largest Wingspan: marabou stork

Smallest: bee hummingbird

Heaviest Flighted: great bustard

FACT 5 **The Not-So-Modern Decimal System** was the invention of the Hindus, around 800 A.D. They invented the sign for zero, too!

In the decimal system, place values are based on groups of 10. Whenever you have 10 of a certain place value, write it as 1 in the next highest place value. When you read a number, always begin with the largest place value. We read 5,632,451.5 as "five million, six hundred thirty-two thousand, four hundred fifty-one and five-tenths."

FACT 6 **Ten Numerals Are All You'll Ever Need** to write in the decimal system.

That's because the numerals 0 through 9 can be combined to stand for other numbers. In the decimal system, each place has a value 10 times greater than the place to its right.

1,234.321

thousands	hundreds	tens	ones	decimal point	tenths	hundredths	thousandths
1	2	3	4	.	3	2	1

FACT 7

Neck and Neck. The human neck has exactly the same number of neck bones as the giraffe, even though a giraffe's neck is 18 times longer!

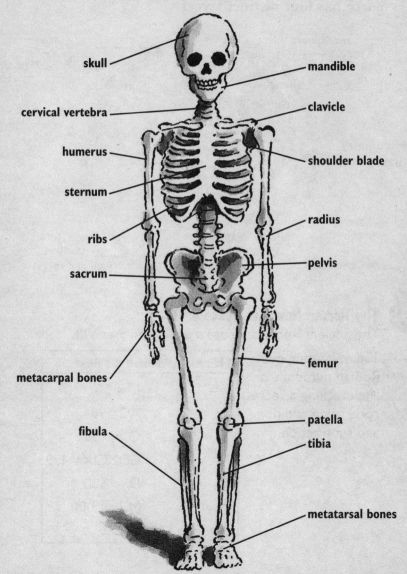

skull

mandible

cervical vertebra

clavicle

humerus

shoulder blade

sternum

radius

ribs

pelvis

sacrum

femur

metacarpal bones

patella

fibula

tibia

metatarsal bones

FACT 8

Is Anybody Out There? Scientists believe Earth was formed more than 4 billion years ago but there was no life at all for the first billion years.

Earth has four distinct layers.

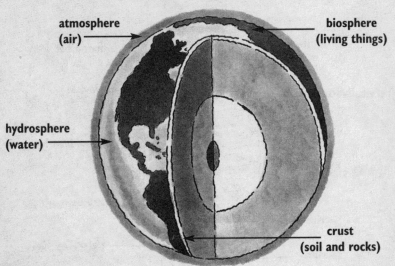

atmosphere (air)

biosphere (living things)

hydrosphere (water)

crust (soil and rocks)

FACT 9

The Roman Numeral System.

The ancient Romans wrote 4 as IIII and 9 as VIIII.

Today, figuring out Roman numerals is like cracking a secret code using addition and subtraction.

Here are some basics:	
I = 1	L = 50
IV = 4	XC=90
V = 5	C = 100
VI = 6	CDXCIX=499
IX = 9	D = 500
X = 10	M = 1,000
XXVII=27	

FACT 10

A **"Pitcher"** is worth a thousand words. A brave woman named Mary McCauley helped General Washington in a battle at Monmouth, New Jersey, in 1778. She carried water to tired and thirsty soldiers, including her husband. When he became exhausted from the heat, she stepped in and continued firing his cannon! We remember her today by her nickname, Molly Pitcher.

FACT 11

What Did You Invent Today, President Jefferson?

President Thomas Jefferson invented dozens of gadgets and machines, from a revolving music stand to a new kind of plow for farming. Thomas Jefferson, our third president, served two terms from 1801 to 1809. While president, Jefferson acquired the Louisiana Territory from Napoleon, doubling the size of the United States.

FACT 12 Meet a Most Remarkable Number: Pi or π

The circumference of a circle is the distance around it. To figure out the circumference, multiply the diameter of the circle (the distance across it through the center) by pi. Pi, or π, is equal to 22/7, or about 3.14.

To figure out the area of a circle, use this special equation: $a = \pi r^2$.

Pi's my name, circumference is my game!

diameter

circumference

FACT 13 Colossal Fossil.

The largest and most complete Tyrannosaurus rex ever found was in the badlands of South Dakota in 1990. Nicknamed Sue, the fossil is 42 feet long and 13 feet tall at the hips.

Fossils are traces or outlines of plants and animals that lived millions of years ago. Most fossils are found in rock, though traces of plant and animal life are sometimes found in tree sap, glaciers, tar pits, and peat beds.

Ten Commonly Misspelled Words.

accompany

believe

broccoli

congratulations

February

judgment

neighbor

occurred

rhythm

separately

1. **Spelling Rule for Silent or final e.** If a word ends with a silent e, drop the e before adding a suffix that begins with a vowel. Do not drop the silent e before adding a suffix that begins with a consonant. Watch out for exceptions to the rule!

2. **Spelling Rule for Words with ie or ei.** *I* before e, except after *c*, or when sounding like *a*, as in *neighbor* and *weigh*.

3. **Spelling Rule for Final y.** If a word ends in a consonant followed by a y, change the y to *i* before adding a suffix. For example, *accompany* becomes *accompanies*. If a word ends in y with a vowel before it, do not change the y to *i* before adding suffixes or other endings.

FACT 15

Hear Ye, Hear Ye: The Thirteen Original States of The United States of America did not include Vermont and Maine. They were considered part of Massachusetts.

The thirteen original states, in the order they ratified the Constitution, are: **Delaware, Pennsylvania, New Jersey, Georgia, Connecticut, Massachusetts, Maryland, South Carolina, New Hampshire, Virginia, New York, North Carolina,** and **Rhode Island.**

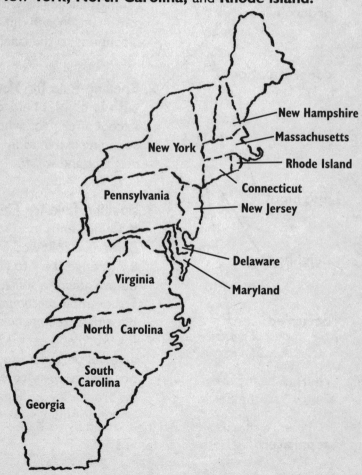

FACT 16

That's a Lot of DNA. It would take about 9.5 years to read out loud, without stopping, all the DNA information present in one person.

The nucleus in a cell contains small parts called chromosomes. Every human cell contains 46 chromosomes, 23 from each parent. The material in each chromosome that carries the information is called deoxyribonucleic acid, or DNA. The DNA molecule looks like a twisted ladder, known as the double helix.

Did You Know? The instructions in the DNA are called genes. Genes are what determine eye color, hair color, whether or not you can roll your tongue, or if you're good at sports. Plant genes determine such traits as height, shape of leaves, and flower color.

FACT 17

Area . . . It's What's Inside.

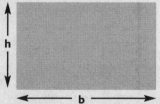

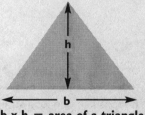

b x h = area of a rectangle

b x h = area of a parallelogram

$$\frac{b \times h}{2} = \text{area of a triangle}$$

To calculate the area of any parallelogram, multiply the base by the height.

To measure the area of a triangle, multiply its base by its height—and then divide by 2.

Say Cheese, President Washington! George Washington did not smile very much because by the time he was 57, he had lost all of his teeth. He had dentures, or false teeth, made out of wood, ivory, and even cow's teeth!

George Washington was the first elected president of the United States of America. He served two consecutive terms, from 1789 to 1797.

CHEESE?

There Are Right Angles Everywhere except in the East Building of the National Gallery of Art in Washington, D.C. It was designed with acute and obtuse angles to fit an odd-shaped site!

When two lines meet, they form an angle. The point where they meet is called the vertex. Angles are measured in degrees. Here are examples of some angles:

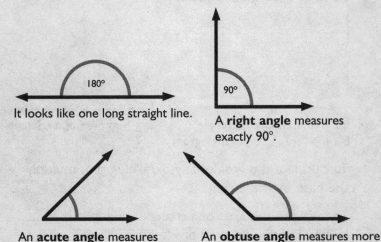

180°
It looks like one long straight line.

90°
A **right angle** measures exactly 90°.

An **acute angle** measures more than 0° but less than 90°.

An **obtuse angle** measures more than 90° but less than 180°.

FACT 20

U.S. Customary System vs. Metric System: Useful Conversions

I centimeter (cm) = .3937 inch
I inch (in) = 2.54 centimeters
I foot (ft) = .3048 meter
I meter (m) = 39.37 inches or 1.094 yards
I yard (yd) = .9144 meter
I kilometer (km) = .621 mile
I mile (mi) = 1.609 kilometers
I acre = .405 hectare
I hectare (ha) = 2.471 acres
I fluid ounce (fl oz) = 29.574 milliliters
I quart (qt) = .946 liter
I liter (l) = 1.057 quarts
I gram (g) = .035 ounce
I ounce (oz) = 28.35 grams
I kilogram (kg) = 2.205 pounds
I pound (lb) = .4535 kilograms

FACT 21

When Is a Sea a Lake? When It's the Caspian.

The Caspian Sea is a lake because it's landlocked, or completely surrounded by land. Here are the five largest natural lakes in the world:

LAKE	CONTINENT	APPROXIMATE AREA
1. Caspian Sea	Asia/Europe	143,250 square miles
2. Lake Superior	North America	31,700 square miles
3. Lake Victoria	Africa	26,828 square miles
4. Lake Huron	North America	23,010 square miles
5. Lake Michigan	North America	22,300 square miles

FACT 22

Rounding and Estimation . . . An Up and Down Relationship.
Estimation is smart guessing that helps you do math without pen, paper, or calculator. To estimate, you have to round numbers to make it easier to do the work.

PET SUPPLIES	PRICES	PRICES ROUNDED
fish tank	$ 9.99	$10.00
net	$ 2.49	$ 2.50
fish food	$ .89	$ .90
heat lamp	$ 6.99	$ 7.00
TOTAL	$20.36	$20.40

To round whole numbers, make a zero of every digit to the right of the given place. Rounding 356 to the nearest tens place becomes 360.

To round decimal numbers, drop the digits to the right of the given place. Rounding .428 to the nearest hundredths place becomes .43

General Rounding Rules. When you estimate, round down from numbers under 5. Round up from numbers 5 or greater.

FACT 23

What's Shakin'?
About 900 earthquakes occur every hour. Most of these are very minor and probably can't be felt by humans.

Earthquakes are sudden violent shifting movements in the earth's crust. They are caused when the tectonic plates that make up the earth's surface collide, separate, or scrape against each other.

Parts of Speech

Noun: A person, place, or thing.

Pronoun: A noun substitute.
    personal subject pronouns: I, you, he, she, it, we, they.
    personal object pronouns: me, him, her, us, them.
    possessive subject pronouns: my, your, his, her, its, our, their, whose.
    possessive object pronouns: mine, yours, his, hers, ours, theirs.

Article: A word that modifies a noun, such as *the*, *a*, and *an*.

Adjective: A word that describes a noun or pronoun.

Verb: An action word.

Adverb: A word that modifies a verb or adjective; a lot of adverbs end in *-ly*, which makes them easy to recognize.

Conjunction: A word that links words and phrases, such as *and*, *or*, *but*, and *because*.

Preposition: A word that shows the relationship between two or more nouns, such as *behind*, *over*, *under*, and *through*.

Interjection: A word or phrase that stands alone to express emotion, such as *Wow!*, *Oops!*, *Hooray!*, and *Yuck!*

Interjection	Article	Adjective	Noun	Adverb	Verb	Adjective	Noun

Wow! The new backpack easily holds five books,

Conjunction	Personal Subject Pronoun	Verb	Article	Noun	Preposition	Possessive Subject Pronoun	Noun	Adverb

and it has a pocket for my calculator, too.

17

FACT 25

It's Alive! Your Blood Is Alive! That's because blood is made up of living cells. In one tiny drop of blood there are 250,000,000 red blood cells!

Blood is made up of red blood cells, white blood cells, platelets, and plasma. The red blood cells carry the oxygen. The white blood cells fight infection and disease. Platelets are tiny bits of cells that help stop bleeding. Plasma is the liquid part of blood that carries nutrients to the rest of the body.

FACT 26

Check Out the Volume of These Solids— They're 3-D, Man!

Always Express Volume in Cubic Terms

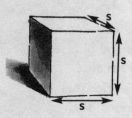

Volume of Cube = S^3

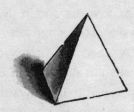

Volume of Pyramid = $\dfrac{\text{area of base (B) x h}}{3}$

Volume of Cylinder = area of base (B) x h

Volume of Cone = $\dfrac{\text{area of base (B) x h}}{3}$

Volume of Sphere = $\dfrac{4 \pi r^3}{3}$

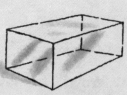

Volume of Rectangular Prism = l x w x h

That's a Lot of Diapers, President Tyler!

President John Tyler had 15 children altogether.

John Tyler was our tenth president. He became president when William Henry Harrison died after only 32 days in office. Tyler served from 1841 to 1845. While he was president, he arranged for the first American trade mission to China and expanded the Monroe Doctrine to include Hawaii.

 FACT 28

You're Right on the Mark!

Comma ,
I got a video game, a CD,
and a robot for my birthday.

Quotation Marks " "
My father said, "This
robot can walk and talk."

Exclamation Mark !
Wow! A robot is a cool
gift to receive.

Semicolon ;
Come to my house; bring your
game controller with you.

Colon :
I have these chores to do first:
clean my room, walk the dog,
and take out the garbage.

FACT 29 **It Keeps on Pumping!** The human heart beats about 100,000 times, and pumps 2,000 gallons of blood through 100,000 miles of organic tubing . . . in one day!

Right Atrium (Upper Right Chamber)

Left Atrium (Upper Left Chamber)

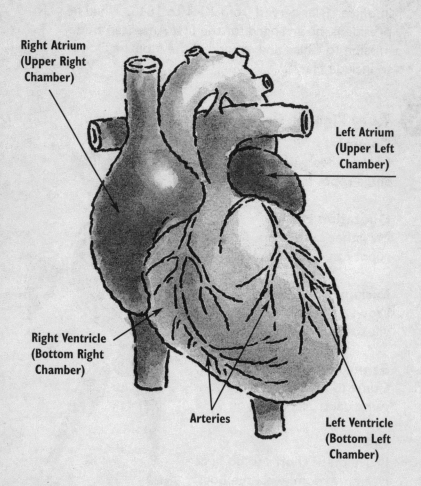

Right Ventricle (Bottom Right Chamber)

Arteries

Left Ventricle (Bottom Left Chamber)

30 **Take a Deep Breath.** In a resting position, a healthy person inhales and exhales about 16 times a minute.

The respiratory system delivers oxygen to body systems and gets rid of unnecessary carbon dioxide.

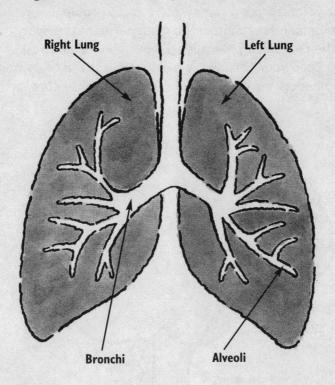

Right Lung

Left Lung

Bronchi

Alveoli

Did You Know? Your left lung is slightly smaller than your right lung!

FACT 31

The Brain is Boss. Your brain controls just about everything your body does.

Think of the brain as a team. The largest player is the cerebrum. It is the thinking part of the brain. It lets you play video games, solve math problems, and remember your mother's birthday. The next player is the cerebellum. Because of your cerebellum, you can keep your balance. Another player is the brain stem. It connects the rest of the brain to the spinal cord.

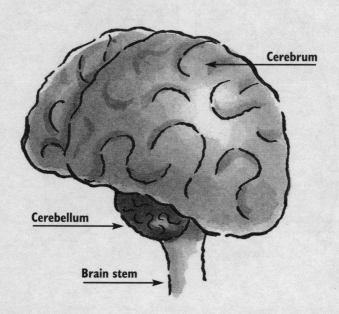

Cerebrum

Cerebellum

Brain stem

32 **The Five Kingdoms.** Living things are often grouped by their kingdom. The kingdoms are: animals, plants, fungus organisms, protists, and monerans. In which kingdom do you belong?

33 **Welcome to My Pad.** An ecosystem is a community of plants and animals interacting with one another and with their environment. The food chain helps to keep the ecosystem up and running. In a simple food chain, plants are eaten by animals, which are eaten by other animals.

34 **Percent Means "Out of 100."** Instead of saying "90 out of 100 students are in the music program," we can say "90% of the students are in the music program."

Here are three ways to write the same thing: 90% = 90/100 = 0.90. We can find any percent of a given number by changing the percent to a decimal and multiplying.

> **Did You Know?** There's an easy way to find 10% of a number without multiplying. Just move the decimal point in the number left by one place.
>
> 10% of 643 = 64.3
>
> 10% of 18 = 1.8
>
> 10% of 21,924 = 2,192.4

35 **The Top Five Most-Spoken Languages in the World Today Are:**

1. Mandarin Chinese — 1 billion speakers
2. English — 700 million speakers
3. Hindi — 497 million speakers
4. Spanish — 293 million speakers
5. Russian — 280 million speakers

> Ni Hao
>
> **Hello**
>
> Namasté
>
> Hola
>
> Zdravstvuite

36 **How About a "H.U.G." President Grant?** President Grant's first name was really Hiram, but he was embarrassed by his initials, H.U.G., so he changed his name!

Ulysses S. Grant, our eighteenth president, was a great military leader who led his army to victory during the Civil War. He served two consecutive terms from 1869 to 1877.

37 **Travel by Magnet.** Homing pidgeons and whales use the earth's magnetic poles to navigate.

Earth's magnetic field is produced by electric currents generated by metals found naturally in Earth's outer core. Scientists believe Earth behaves like one big round magnet. The point where the magnetic field lines leave Earth's surface pointing straight up is called the Magnetic South Pole; the point where the magnetic field lines point straight down is the Magnetic North Pole.

FACT 38

What do EPCOT, LASER, and PIN All Have in Common? They are Acronyms. Acronyms are formed from the first letters of words in phrases or titles. How many of these do you recognize?

EPCOT	Experimental Prototype Community of Tomorrow
LASER	light amplification by stimulated emission of radiation
NATO	North Atlantic Treaty Organization (peacekeeping alliance)
PIN	Personal Identification Number (used for bank cards, credit cards, etc.)
RAM	random-access memory (short-term computer memory)
ZIP code	zone improvement plan

FACT 39

Word Alert. When words sound the same, mean different things, and usually have different spellings they are called **homophones**. **Homographs** are words that have the same spellings but have different meanings. **Homonyms** fall into both of these groups!

Call My Cell. Plant cells and animal cells share parts in common, but only plant cells have cell walls and chloroplast.

Cells are the tiny building blocks of life. All living things are made up of cells. These drawings show an animal cell and a plant cell.

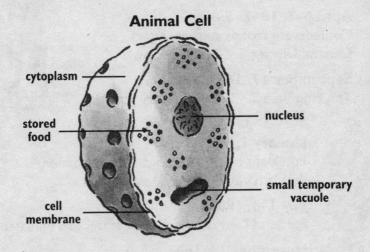

Animal Cell

- cytoplasm
- stored food
- cell membrane
- nucleus
- small temporary vacuole

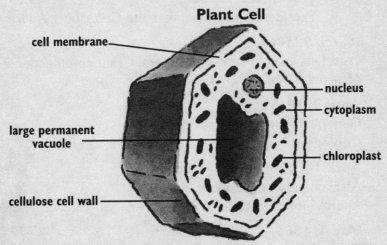

Plant Cell

- cell membrane
- large permanent vacuole
- cellulose cell wall
- nucleus
- cytoplasm
- chloroplast

FACT 41 The Civil War Began at Fort Sumter on April 12, 1861.

Here are ten important events of the American Civil War:

July 21, 1861 FIRST BATTLE OF BULL RUN
The Union is defeated. Confederate general
Thomas Jackson earns the nickname
"Stonewall" Jackson.

April 6–7, 1862 SHILOH
Confederate troops surprise attack
General Ulysses S. Grant's troops.

September 17, 1862 ANTIETAM
The bloodiest day in U.S. military history;
256,000 soldiers lose their lives.

January 1, 1863
President Lincoln issues the Emancipation
Proclamation, freeing all slaves.

July 1–3, 1863
Battle of Gettysburg; Confederates are defeated.

November 19, 1863
President Lincoln delivers the Gettysburg Address.

March 9, 1864
President Lincoln appoints General Grant commander
of all armies of the United States.

April 9, 1865
General Robert E. Lee surrenders his
Confederate army to General Ulysses S. Grant.

April 14, 1865
Assassination of President Lincoln;
Andrew Johnson becomes President.

May 4, 1865
Final surrender of Confederate army.

Talk to Your Plant. It Might Help It Grow!

Why? When we exhale, we release carbon dioxide into the air. Carbon dioxide helps plants make their own food.

In a process called photosynthesis, plants use the sun's energy, carbon dioxide from the air, and water from the soil to produce their own food. During this reaction, the plant gives off oxygen, which is what we need to breathe.

Did You Know? The word "chlorophyll" comes from two Greek words: "chlor," meaning green, and "phyllo," meaning leaf.

But chlorophyll can be found in other parts of a plant besides its leaves. Chlorophyll makes cells appear green. This important molecule traps the energy plants need to make food.

Surprising, but Probable. If you toss a coin 200 times, either heads or tails will come up 6 or more times in a row!

Probability is a number used to describe the chance that something will happen. If you toss a coin, a result of heads is one chance in two (the other result is tails). In math, we express probability with a ratio, like 1:2, or a percentage, 50%. So, no matter how many times you toss a coin, the probability that it will be heads is 1:2. You can count on it!

FACT 44 — Art Styles of the Rich and Famous.

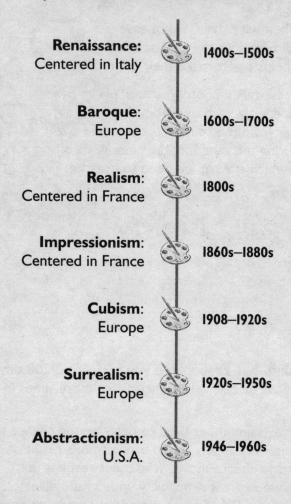

Renaissance: Centered in Italy — 1400s–1500s

Baroque: Europe — 1600s–1700s

Realism: Centered in France — 1800s

Impressionism: Centered in France — 1860s–1880s

Cubism: Europe — 1908–1920s

Surrealism: Europe — 1920s–1950s

Abstractionism: U.S.A. — 1946–1960s

FACT 45 — Roy G. Biv, a.k.a. Rainbow Man. A ray of sunlight actually produces a spectrum of seven colors. You can remember the visible spectrum—red, orange, yellow, green, blue, indigo, violet—by remembering the name of one colorful fellow, ROY G. BIV.

FACT 46

111,111,111 x 111,111,111 = 12,345,678,987,654,321

You read the answer:

> twelve quadrillion
> three hundred forty-five trillion
> six hundred seventy-eight billion
> nine hundred eighty-seven million
> six hundred fifty-four thousand
> three hundred twenty-one.

FACT 47

Catch My Drift. About 200 million years ago there was only one continent. Scientists call it Pangaea. Over time, the movement of Earth's crust broke the thin surface to form the continents we know today. That movement is called continental drift.

The continents are moving right at this moment, but very, very slowly. In another 200 million years, Earth may look completely different again.

The movement and breaking of Earth's crust is known as plate tectonics. This movement also forms mountains, volcanoes, and causes earthquakes.

FACT 48

The Major Scale Is the Backbone of Western Music. It is a series of eight consecutive notes that follow a pattern of half and whole steps. You might know it as the famous do-re-mi-fa-so-la-ti-do syllables.

Why Didn't the Prefix and Suffix Want To Leave? Because They Got Attached to Words!

Prefixes attach to the beginning of a word to form a new word. Suffixes attach to the end of a word to form a new word.

PREFIXES		SUFFIXES	
un-	unpack	-ly	sadly
co-	coordinate	-tion	production
sub-	submarine	-ful	hopeful
inter-	interview	-less	careless
de-	destruction	-er	teacher

It Feels Like a Rock and looks like a plant, but coral is actually a colony of tiny animals. In hard coral, what we see is the outer skeleton of the tiny, fragile animal. And only the thin outermost part of coral is alive.

All animals belong to one of two large groups—vertebrates or invertebrates. A vertebrate is an animal with a backbone. You are a vertebrate. An invertebrate is an animal with no backbone. Coral is an invertebrate.

Karaoke Means "Empty Orchestra" in Japanese.

The instruments of the orchestra can be divided up into four types: strings, woodwinds, brass, and percussion.

52 The last slaves in America were freed in 1865,

two and a half years after President Lincoln issued
the Emancipation Proclamation.

Important civil rights events to remember:

1909—National Association for the Advancement
of Colored People (NAACP) is formed.

1942—Congress of Racial Equality (CORE) is founded.

1947—Jackie Robinson becomes the first black player
in major league baseball.

1954—In *Brown* vs. *Board of Education*, the Supreme
Court bans segregation in public schools.

1955—Rosa Parks refuses to give up her seat on the
bus to a white person; desegregation of buses
in Montgomery, Alabama, begins.

1963—Martin Luther King, Jr., gives "I Have a Dream"
speech in March on Washington.

53 The "Underground Railroad" Was Not Underground

or a Railroad. It was a secret network of people who
risked their lives before and during the Civil War to
lead slaves to freedom.

Harriet Tubman was a "conductor" on the "underground
railroad" who helped her relatives and other slaves flee
to the North. She used many disguises and is credited
with leading more than 300 slaves to freedom.

Get the Point of Intersecting Lines? The point is that there's only one point!

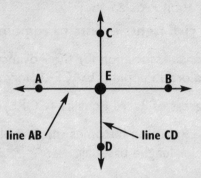

Intersecting lines are in the same plane and pass through each other at one point. Some streets in your neighborhood form intersecting lines. Where the streets meet is called an intersection.

Parallel Lines Helped to Figure Out How Big Earth is . . . More Than 2,000 Years Ago! A scientist called Erastothenes calculated the circumference of Planet Earth using the parallel light rays from the sun.

Parallel lines lie within the same plane and are always the same distance apart. They continue in the same plane and they never, ever touch. Parallel lines are all around us: on the playground, at the bowling alley, and in your home.

Rock On, with Toothpaste. Toothpaste is made up of a sedimentary rock called limestone. When you clean your teeth, a powdered form of limestone helps to remove bits of food. So brush on! And don't worry if you swallow a little—it's harmless.

Scientists place rocks in three classes, according to the way they are formed: **igneous**, **sedimentary**, and **metamorphic**.

Igneous rock
When the magma from a volcano cools, it forms igneous rock. Granite is an igneous rock.

Sedimentary rock
When layers of minerals or decayed plants are squeezed together by water pressure, sedimentary rock forms. Sandstone is a sedimentary rock.

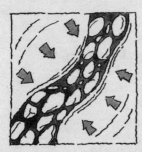

Metamorphic rock
Forces within the earth, such as pressure or temperature, change igneous or sedimentary rock into another form. A rock that has been changed is called a metamorphic rock. Marble is a metamorphic rock.

57 Weathering and Erosion. Partners in Time. The base of the Grand Canyon in Arizona is made up of sedimentary rock that is 1.7 billion years old.

Rain, wind, and ice can cause rocks to break apart and move away from the parent rock. When rocks are broken down into smaller pieces the process is called weathering. Once rocks are weathered, they may move from their original location. This action is called erosion.

Did You Know? Talc and diamond have something in common. They are both minerals.

Minerals are the building blocks of rocks. They are identified by their hardness, based on a scale of one to ten. One is the softest mineral, talc. Ten is the hardest mineral, diamond.

58 There's Nothing Improper About Fractions. $^{13}/_4 = 3^1/_4$

To add fractions, the fractions must have common denominators. Simply add the numerators. The denominator will remain the same.

$$^1/_5 + {}^2/_5 = {}^3/_5$$

To subtract fractions, the fractions must also have common denominators.

$$^7/_9 - {}^4/_9 = {}^3/_9$$

To add and subtract mixed numerals, rewrite the numerals as improper fractions.

$$2^1/_5 - 1^3/_{10} = 2^2/_{10} - 1^3/_{10}$$

$$^{22}/_{10} - {}^{13}/_{10} = {}^9/_{10}$$

59 **What a High Bid for a Grid!** In 1999, a person paid $398,500 for a map of Samuel de Champlain's voyage, dated 1612.

Today we use grids to locate things from stadium seats to city buildings to search-and-rescue operations. A grid is made up of intersecting lines. The horizontal line is the x-axis. The vertical line is the y-axis. The location of every point on a grid is expressed by a pair of numbers written like this: (x, y).

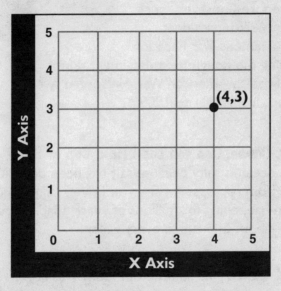

60 **How Deep Is the Ocean?** On average, it is a little more than two miles. But the deepest ocean trench, the Mariana Trench in the Pacific Ocean, is nearly 7 miles deep. Compare that to Mount Everest, which is only 6 miles high!

The ocean floor has the same features as our above-water landscape—canyons, plateaus, ridges, and mountain ranges—and there are plants and animals that have adapted to the cold, dark conditions.

Fact 61 Let the Good Times Roll, President Roosevelt!

President Theodore Roosevelt's family had a lot of fun while living in the White House. His six children rode bicycles in the halls and also held roller-skating contests.

Theodore Roosevelt, our twenty-sixth president, was a famous war hero for leading the Rough Rider Regiment during the Spanish-American War. He served two terms, from 1901 to 1909.

Fact 62 Hey, Ocean, Can You Lend Me a Cup of Salt?

The ocean is salty because salt has been deposited in it from rocks, soil, water, and rivers. Since this has been happening for millions of years, that's a lot of salt—about one cup in every gallon!

Fact 63 Wild Winds.

The summit of Mount Washington in New Hampshire is known for its harsh weather. In 1934, winds reached a world record of 231 miles per hour—and these gusts were not part of a storm!

Wind is moving air. It can travel in huge spirals up and down. It also moves horizontally. These movements cause many different wind patterns across the planet.

FACT 64 Colony of Ants and Other Collective Nouns.

Bale of cotton

Batch of cookies

Company of soldiers

Clump of grass

Gaggle of geese

Galaxy of stars

Nest of snakes
  (also spies, bowls)

Pride of lions

Shock of wheat
  (also hair)

Stack of pancakes

Did You Know? Groups of nouns (persons, animals, and things) often have a special word to name the group. These words are called collective nouns.

FACT 65 Lighter Than Air? The miles of air above us actually weigh a lot—about 15 pounds of pressure on every square inch of your body!

The weight of the air pressing down on Earth's surface is called atmospheric pressure.

When Can a Math Teacher Solve a Vision Problem? When It's Di-Vision!

Division problems can be written like this:

$$32 \div 4 = 8$$

dividend   divisor   quotient

or like this:

$$8 \text{ — quotient}$$
$$\text{divisor — } 4 \overline{)\, 32} \text{ — dividend}$$

Many numbers do not fit evenly into other numbers. We say they are not evenly divisible. The number left over is called the remainder.

Hurricane Mitch was the deadliest hurricane in the twentieth century. It pounded Central America, beginning on October 26, 1998, killing more than 11,000 people.

Let's untwist some storm words. Cyclones are warm-weather systems surrounded by cooler air. When the winds exceed 75 miles per hour and originate in the Atlantic Ocean, off the western coast of Africa, the cyclone is called a hurricane. A tornado is a cyclone that occurs over land. Tornadoes bring about the highest wind speeds on Earth, upward of 311 miles per hour. Now, that's a twister!

FACT 68

The Euro Became the Common European Currency in 1999. Here are some other world currencies:

U.S.A. = Dollars

Great Britain = Pounds

China = Yuan Renminbi

Japan = Yen

South Africa = Rand

India = Rupees

Israel = New Shekels

Turkey = Liras

Brazil = Reais

Argentina = Pesos

Did You Know? Paper money is actually made out of rags! Rag fibers made from cotton are stronger than paper fibers. That's why a dollar bill doesn't fall apart when you accidentally wash it along with your jeans.

American money is based on the decimal system. We add, subtract, multiply, and divide money the same way we do any decimal numbers.

69 **The Truth About Myths.** Ancient civilizations gave names to gods and goddesses who, they believed, performed different jobs. For example:

Zeus: king of the gods; also god of the sky and thunder

Apollo: god of the sun; also god of music

Athena: goddess of wisdom

Aphrodite: goddess of love

Ares: god of war

Mythology is a collection of stories that helps to explain our beliefs and our history. Many words we use today come from mythology.

Zeus

Matter, Matter Everywhere! Matter can exist as solid, liquid, or gas. Water is the only natural substance known to exist in all three states: ice, water, or vapor.

Matter is anything that has both volume and mass. Volume is the amount of space the stuff takes up. Mass is the amount of stuff there is.

A Whopper of a Wave. The biggest tsunami ever recorded occurred off the volcanic island of Krakatau, Indonesia, in 1883. Its height was more than 120 feet tall. That's about as tall as a twelve-story building!

Tsunamis are large, rapidly moving walls of water, triggered by a major disturbance of the ocean floor, such as an earthquake or landslide.

Did You Know? Tsunamis are not tidal waves. Tidal waves are caused by the forces of the moon, sun, and planets upon the tides as well as the wind as it moves over water.

Personification in Writing Is Making Something Not Human Behave Like a Human. "The wind sang a sad and slow melody," is a personification.

FACT 73

A Heavenly System. The sun is the center of the solar system. That means the planets revolve around it. Here's a saying that will help you remember the order of the planets from the sun, beginning with Mercury: **M**y **V**ery **E**ducated **M**other **J**ust **S**howed **U**s **N**ine **P**lanets.

Did You Know? The solar system is about 9.3 billion miles across. The sun makes up more than 99 percent of the solar system's mass. All the planets put together make up less than 1 percent!

My	●	**Mercury**
Very	○	**Venus**
Educated	◉	**Earth**
Mother	○	**Mars**
Just		**Jupiter**
Showed		**Saturn**
Us	◎	**Uranus**
Nine	●	**Neptune**
Planets	○	**Pluto**

On Behalf of Graphs . . . There Are Four You Should Know.

Bar Graphs Compare Data

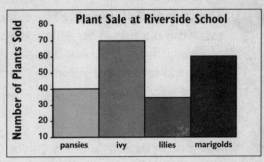

Plant Sale at Riverside School

Number of Plants Sold

80, 70, 60, 50, 40, 30, 20, 10

pansies   ivy   lilies   marigolds

Line Graph Show Changes on Data

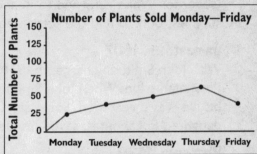

Number of Plants Sold Monday—Friday

Total Number of Plants

150, 125, 100, 75, 50, 25, 0

Monday   Tuesday   Wednesday   Thursday   Friday

Pictographs show data in a small space using icons

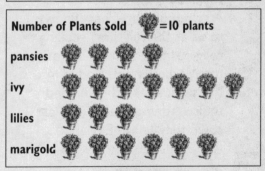

Number of Plants Sold 🌼 = 10 plants

pansies

ivy

lilies

marigold

Circle graphs are circles divided into parts that show proportions or numbers of data.

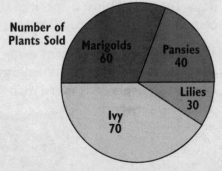

Number of Plants Sold

Marigolds 60

Pansies 40

Lilies 30

Ivy 70

75 The Oldest Settlement.

The explorer Pedro Menendez established a fort in St. Augustine in 1565 for the King of Spain, Philip II. St. Augustine is the oldest continuous European settlement in North America.

Other "New World" Settlements:

Roanoke, 1587

The British established this colony. Four years later, Governor White returned to Roanoke from England with supplies, only to find the settlement had disappeared!

Jamestown, 1607

With John Smith in charge, the settlers traded with the Powhatan tribe. When John Smith would not trade guns, his life was threatened. Some say Chief Powhatan's daughter, Pocahontas, saved his life.

Plymouth, 1620

A group of Christians (known to us as the Pilgrims) seeking religious freedom set sail on the *Mayflower* and landed in Massachusetts. They named their settlement after the last town they left in England.

76 Now, That's Hot!

Just a speck of the sun's hot gas could destroy life up to 99 miles away.

The sun is 93,000,000 miles away from Earth. Even so, the amount of sun energy that reaches Earth's atmosphere is more than 1,370 watts per square meter!

FACT 77

Wind Tries Harder. Humans have harnessed the energy of wind for more than 2,000 years. Until the Industrial Revolution, wind was second to wood as a source of energy.

Scientists and inventors have found ways to harness many different forms of natural energy. Renewable energy sources can be replenished, or made again, in a short period of time. Nonrenewable energy sources cannot be replenished in a short period of time.

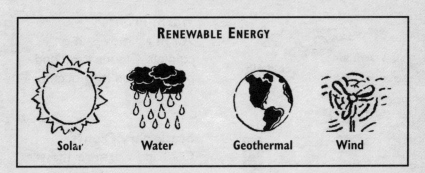

RENEWABLE ENERGY

Solar   Water   Geothermal   Wind

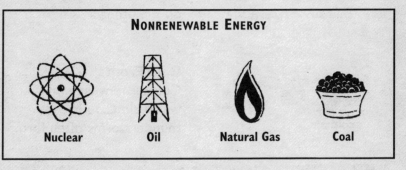

NONRENEWABLE ENERGY

Nuclear   Oil   Natural Gas   Coal

78 **Up Front with the Weather.** When a warm air mass and a cold air mass meet, they do not mix together right away. The edge along which the two masses meet is called a front. Here are the ways fronts react:

cold air

cool air

warm air

Occluded Fronts
A cold front catches up to a warm front, forcing the warm air up.

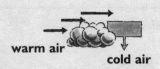

warm air

cold air

Warm Fronts
Warm air moves in on cold air. Clouds form and precipitation may occur.

cold air

warm air

Stationary Fronts
Cold and warm air masses meet, but neither moves on the other.

warm air

cold air

Cold Fronts
Cold air moves in on warm air. Clouds and thunderstorms often form.

Did You Know? Barometers measure air pressure. Rising air pressure usually means the weather will be fair. Falling air pressure may mean a storm is approaching.

FACT 79

Painting Pictures with Words Using Similes and Metaphors.

Similes

Her eyes are as shiny as diamonds.

The house was as quiet as falling snow.

Baby Jill smelled like a spring rain.

Metaphors

The teacher was drowning in test papers.

He is a class clown.

Her eyes were darts peering through the keyhole.

Similes are figures of speech that compare two unlike things using the words *like* or *as*. Metaphors compare two unlike things to show a likeness between them without using the words *like* or *as*.

FACT 80

Hello Madam, I'm Atom.

Atoms are tiny building blocks of matter. They are so tiny that you can't even see them with a microscope. But scientists can weigh them, measure them, and tell them apart. Inside the center of an atom is a nucleus, or core. The nucleus is made up of protons and neutrons. Protons have a positive electrical charge. Neutrons have no charge. Electrons move around the nucleus in electron clouds. The negative charge of electrons is attracted to the positive charge of protons in the nucleus.

FACT 81

When The President Vetoes, Or Rejects, A Bill, Congress May Still Act To Pass The Bill. The U.S. Constitution gives Congress the power to override the President's veto with a two-thirds majority vote of both the House and the Senate.

Our federal government protects our freedoms and prevents the government from abusing power. Here's how it's done:

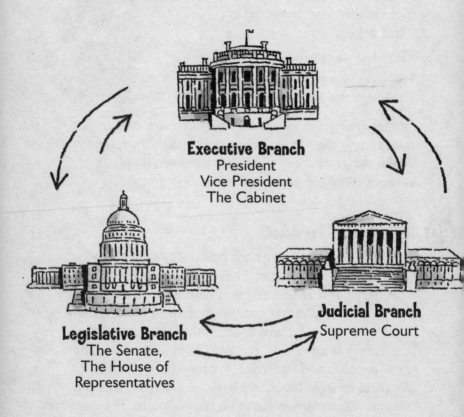

Executive Branch
President
Vice President
The Cabinet

Judicial Branch
Supreme Court

Legislative Branch
The Senate,
The House of
Representatives

82 **A Hot Debate: Heat vs. Temperature.** Which has more heat, a cup of water that is 100°F or a filled bathtub that is 75°F? The bathtub has more heat!

Heat is a form of energy. It moves atoms and molecules. The more energy they take in, the more they move. It would take a lot of heat to raise the temperature of a tub filled with water but it takes only a little heat to raise the temperature of a cup of water.

Temperature is a measure of the average amount of heat of the movement of those atoms and molecules in a volume of matter. The water in the cup was very hot and its temperature was high. The molecules in the cup of water were vibrating very fast. The tub of water was warm, its temperature was lower, and the molecules were vibrating less fast.

Did You Know? The melting point and freezing point of a substance are the same temperature. What happens to it at this temperature depends on whether we add heat to it or take heat from it.

83 **Temperature Is a Matter of Degrees.** In the 1700s, Gabriel Fahrenheit created a thermometer using the degree unit. On the Fahrenheit scale, water freezes at sea level at 32°F (32 degrees Fahrenheit) and boils at 212°F. Anders Celsius created a newer scale, putting the freezing point of water at 0°C (zero degrees Celsius) and the boiling point at 100°C.

Converting Scales of Temperature:

(Celsius temperature x 9/5) + 32 = Fahrenheit temperature

(Fahrenheit temperature − 32) x 5/9 = Celsius temperature

FACT 84

Count on a Cricket to figure out the average temperature in the summer. Count the cricket chirps you hear in 15 seconds and add 39. That number should give you the Fahrenheit temperature outdoors. Now figure it out in Celsius!

FACT 85

Have Seed, Will Travel. A seed must find the right place to grow. Dandelion seeds have built-in parachutes that let them travel on the wind. A dwarf mistletoe can shoot its seeds as far as 50 feet!

Most plants reproduce through seeds. Inside every seed is a tiny new plant, or embryo. Conifers make seeds in cones. Flowering plants make seeds in flowers.

FACT 86

Flower Power. The flower seed is like a lunch box. Inside is food for the new plant and outside is a protective cover.

To make seeds, pollination and fertilization must occur. Pollen is made in the stamen, the "male" part of the flower. Fertilization occurs when pollen enters the ovule, the "female" part of the flower.

FACT 87

The Word Astronaut Comes From Two Greek Roots That Mean "Star Sailor."

America has been involved in modern space exploration since 1961, when Alan Shepard became the first U.S. astronaut in space. Here are other major events in American space exploration:

1962 John H. Glenn, Jr. orbits the earth.

1968 *Apollo 8* orbits the moon 10 times.

1969 Neil Armstrong and Edwin "Buzz" Aldrin, in *Apollo 11,* become the first humans to land on the moon.

1979 *Voyager 2* photographs Jupiter.

1981 First flight of space shuttle *Columbia.*

1983 Aboard space shuttle *Challenger,* Sally Ride becomes the first female U.S. astronaut in space.

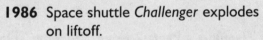

1986 Space shuttle *Challenger* explodes on liftoff.

1989 *Voyager 2* photographs Neptune.

1997 U.S. space probe *Pathfinder* lands on Mars.

2003 Space shuttle *Columbia* explodes during reentry through Earth's atmosphere.

Guess What the Man on the Moon Just Heard? Absolutely Nothing. That's because there is no air on the moon.

Sound vibrations can exist only in things that have mass, such as air, water, and any solid object on this planet.

The Cold Facts: The Average Temperature of the World's Oceans Is About 39°F (4°C). The oceans of the world are:

OCEAN	APPROXIMATE AREA
1. **Pacific**	63.8 million square miles
2. **Atlantic**	31.8 million square miles
3. **Indian**	28.4 million square miles
4. **Southern**	7.8 million square miles
5. **Arctic**	5.4 million square miles

Planning a Party? Here Are Four Things to Include in Your Invitation:

1. Type of event — (birthday party, surprise party, graduation party, and so on)

2. Time of event —

3. Date of event —

4. Place of event —

And don't forget to add *R.S.V.P.* That stands for *répondez s'il vous plaît,* and means *please respond.*

You're Invited to

My Birthday Party

**2:00pm,
Saturday, November 8, 2003**

**My house,
64 Hickory Drive**

**Please r.s.v.p. to
555-6101**

FACT 91

Now Hear This . . . But Only If You're a Dog. Dogs and other animals can hear ultrasonic sounds, which are far above the frequency that humans hear.

To measure frequency, scientists use the hertz unit. One hertz means one vibration per second. Most people can hear sounds with frequencies from about 20 to 20,000 hertz. Many animals are able to hear frequencies far above, as well as below, human range.

FACT 92

The Longest Mountain Range in the World is Located Under the Ocean! The Mid-Ocean Ridge is about 31,000 miles long. It extends from the Arctic Ocean, down the middle of the Atlantic, and winds into the Pacific Ocean.

The longest mountain range above sea level is the Andes, in South America. It is 4,500 miles long.

FACT 93

The "No Sound" Radio Station. Radio stations transmit an electromagnetic wave, not sound.

The radio station encodes a pattern on the wave it transmits, and then our radios decode the pattern and translate the pattern into sound.

Five Parts To a Letter

Heading: Date, your address; if it's a business letter, include the name and address of the person to whom you are writing.

Greeting: May begin with "Dear." Put a comma at the end of the greeting in a friendly letter and a colon in a business letter.

Body: Main part of letter.

Closing: May end with "Your friend" or "Sincerely yours." Remember to capitalize the first word of the closing and put a comma at the end of the closing.

Signature: Sign your name below the closing.

---

11 Shadyside Lane, Beachtown, NY 11223 ·········· **Heading**

July 4, 2004

Jackie Silver
President
Tuffstuff Playgrounds
123 Riverside Drive
Playtown, OH 41254

Dear Ms. Silver: ······································· **Greeting**

I am interested in purchasing playground equipment for my backyard. Please send me your latest catalog. ·········· **Body**

Sincerely yours, ······································· **Closing**

Erika Marascot ······································· **Signature**

95 Famous Classical Composers: Their Works and Quirks

Antonio Vivaldi
(1678–1741)
From: Italy
Work: *The Four Seasons*
Quirk: He was a priest, and often left the altar to jot down musical ideas.

Johann Sebastian Bach (1685–1750)
From: Germany
Work: *The Brandenburg Concertos*
Quirk: He liked vocal music and sang in a choir.

George Frideric Handel
(1685–1759)
From: Germany
Work: *The Messiah*
Quirk: He lost his sight but continued to compose and play organ concertos from memory.

Ludwig van Beethoven
(1770–1827)
From: Germany
Work: *Symphony #5 in C Minor*
Quirk: He threw temper tantrums; was deaf, too, yet still composed.

Wolfgang Amadeus Mozart
(1756–1791)
From: Austria
Work: *The Magic Flute*
Quirk: He invented an imaginary kingdom called Back, of which he was king, and persuaded his servant to map out the cities and villages.

Nifty Fifty: State Nicknames. Can you guess why these names were given?

STATE	NICKNAME	CAPITAL
Alabama	Yellowhammer State	Montgomery
Alaska	"The Last Frontier" and "Land of the Midnight Sun"	Juneau
Arizona	Grand Canyon State; Copper State	Phoenix
Arkansas	Natural State	Little Rock
California	Golden State	Sacramento
Colorado	Centennial State	Denver
Connecticut	Constitution State; Nutmeg State	Hartford
Delaware	First State; Diamond State; "Small Wonder"	Dover
Florida	Sunshine State	Tallahassee
Georgia	Peach State, Empire State of the South	Atlanta
Hawaii	Aloha State	Honolulu
Idaho	Gem State	Boise
Illinois	Prairie State	Springfield
Indiana	Hoosier State	Indianapolis
Iowa	Hawkeye State	Des Moines

STATE	NICKNAME	CAPITAL
Kansas	Sunflower State; Jayhawk State	Topeka
Kentucky	Bluegrass State	Frankfort
Louisiana	Pelican State	Baton Rouge
Maine	Pine Tree State	Augusta
Maryland	Old Line State; Free State	Annapolis
Massachusetts	Bay State; Old Colony State	Boston
Michigan	Wolverine State; Great Lake State	Lansing
Minnesota	North Star State; "Land of 10,000 Lakes"	St. Paul
Mississippi	Magnolia State	Jackson
Missouri	Show-me State	Jefferson City
Montana	Treasure State	Helena
Nebraska	Cornhusker State; Beef State	Lincoln
Nevada	Sagebrush State; Silver State; Battle-born State	Carson City
New Hampshire	Granite State	Concord
New Jersey	Garden State	Trenton
New Mexico	"Land of Enchantment"	Santa Fe
New York	Empire State	Albany

STATE	NICKNAME	CAPITAL
North Carolina	Old North State; Tar Heel State	Raleigh
North Dakota	Sioux State; Flickertail State; Peace Garden State	Bismarck
Ohio	Buckeye State	Columbus
Oklahoma	Sooner State	Oklahoma City
Oregon	Beaver State	Salem
Pennsylvania	Keystone State	Harrisburg
Rhode Island	Ocean State; Plantation State	Providence
South Carolina	Palmetto State	Columbia
South Dakota	Mount Rushmore State; Coyote State	Pierre
Tennessee	Volunteer State	Nashville
Texas	Lone Star State	Austin
Utah	Beehive State	Salt Lake City
Vermont	Green Mountain State	Montpelier
Virginia	Old Dominion State; Mother of States	Richmond
Washington	Evergreen State; Chinook State	Olympia
West Virginia	Mountain State	Charleston
Wisconsin	Badger State	Madison
Wyoming	Equality State	Cheyenne

97 When Is the Tallest Mountain in the World an Island? When It's Mauna Kea, an Inactive Volcanic Island in Hawaii! When measured from ocean floor to summit, this island stands 33,465 feet tall!

Any piece of land that rises quickly to 1,000 feet higher than the land around it can be considered a mountain. The world's highest mountain above sea level is Mount Everest at about 29,028 feet.

98 Refraction Fun. When you place a straw in a glass of water and look at it through the glass, the straw will

look broken. This broken or bending of light is called refraction.

Light travels faster through air than other substances. When a light ray passes at an oblique or slanted angle from one kind of material to another, its path appears to bend. That is why the straw appears broken where it hits the water.

FACT 99

Be a Scientist . . . or at Least Write Like One!

Follow this form used by scientists.

hypothesis	**experiment**	**conclusion**
states what your experiment is designed to test	lists materials, procedure, and results	states what your experiment proves

Hypothesis: A magnet has an invisible force around it.

Materials:

1 bar magnet

1 compass

1 sheet of paper

Procedure:

1. Place the magnet in the center of a sheet of paper.

2. Put the compass near one end of the magnet. Let the needle stop moving. Note the direction of the needle. Lift the compass and draw an arrow in the same direction as the compass needle.

3. Move the compass toward the middle of the magnet. When the needle settles, note its direction and draw an arrow as before.

4. Repeat this as you move from end to end at least 3 times. Explore both above and below the magnet.

Results: The arrow moved as the compass was placed all around the magnet.

Conclusion: The magnet caused the compass arrow to move, proving there is an invisible magnetic field around a magnet.

FACT 100

Around the Seventh Century A.D., the Maya built a 600-foot-long bridge with massive concrete piers, a rope-cable suspension system, towers, and a bed of hard wooden planks.

Civilizations of the Americas developed sophisticated cities, large temples, and pyramids. Many of these ruins can still be seen today.

1500 B.C. – 200 A.D.   The Olmec lived along the Gulf of Mexico.

2000 B.C. – 1460 A.D.   The Maya lived in the Yucatán peninsula in Central America.

1200 – 1521 A.D.   The Aztec lived in what is now central and southern Mexico.

1200 – 1534 A.D.   The Inca lived in the Andes mountains of South America.

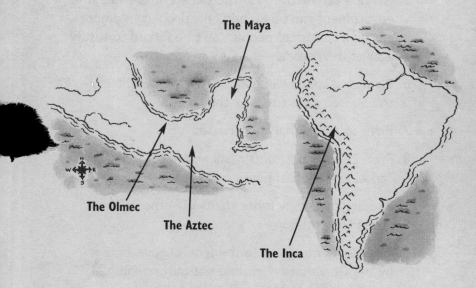

The Maya

The Olmec

The Aztec

The Inca

Know Your Rights! The Bill of Rights started out as 12 amendments but the State Legislatures only adopted 10.

The Bill of Rights were the first 10 amendments added to the American Constitution in 1791. Some people (and states) felt these rights needed to be added to protect their freedom.

1. Freedom of speech and the press; freedom to gather in public; freedom to ask the government for help; the government can't declare an official religion for the country.

2. Right to keep and bear arms.

3. The government can't take over people's houses to put soldiers there.

4. Protection from unreasonable search and seizure.

5. No one can be tried for the same crime twice; the government can't take personal property without paying a fair price; people can't be forced to testify against themselves.

6. Right to a speedy and fair trial by jury; right to counsel; right to know the charge.

7. Right to a jury trial in civil cases.

8. Protection against unfair bail and fines, and against "cruel and unusual punishment."

9. People have many more rights than those listed in the Constitution.

10. All powers not given to the federal government by the Constitution go automatically to the people or the states.